GETTING TO KNOW

ITALY

Cinzia Mariella

PASSPORT BOOKS
a division of *NTC Publishing Group*
Lincolnwood, Illinois USA

Editor: Karin Fancett (Format Publishing Services)
Design: Tony Truscott
        Edward Kinsey
Illustrations: Hayward Art Group
Consultant: Keith Lye

Photographs: Chris Fairclough, ZEFA, BBC
Hulton Picture Library, Benetton (Fantomax), J.
Allan Cash, Design Council/Victoria and Albert
Museum, Zoë Dominic, Ente Nazionale Italiano
per il Turismo (ENIT), Ferrari, Fiat, Gucci,
Keystone Press Agency, Italian Embassy
(London), Italian Institute, The Mansell
Collection, Cinzia Mariella, The National Gallery,
Popperfoto, Zanussi

Front cover: Chris Fairclough, ZEFA
Back cover: Chris Fairclough

Contents

Introduction

Italy is an ancient country situated in southern Europe, and surrounded on three sides by the Mediterranean Sea. Also included within its borders are the two large Mediterranean islands of Sicily and Sardinia. Italy's scenery is extremely varied, ranging from high mountain ranges such as the Alps and Apennines to rich pastureland and fertile plains.

A democratic republic, Italy's official name is *Repubblica Italiana* (Italian Republic). The country has enjoyed a long and important role in shaping history and continues to play a leading part in world affairs today. Italy was a founder member of the European Economic Community (EEC) and also of the North Atlantic Treaty Organization (NATO). Italy is also a major industrial and agricultural nation and the Italians have succeeded in mixing traditional methods with new technology.

Italy is a land of great beauty, changing landscapes and rich cultural diversity, whose history, traditions and artistic expression have blended to create a uniqueness that could only be Italian.

Above: Traditional festivals are still common in Italy. These horsemen are taking part in the festival of St. Efisio at Cagliari.

Below: Many parts of Italy are a blend of old and new. This modern highway winds past old buildings as it cuts through the outskirts of Genoa.

The land

Mainland Italy is a long, boot-shaped peninsula in the southern part of Europe, that stretches far into the Mediterranean Sea. To the south and west are the large islands of Sicily and Sardinia, as well as other, smaller islands. The Italian coastline is washed by the Ligurian and Tyrrhenian Seas to the west, the Adriatic Sea to the east and the Ionian Sea to the south. In the north, the high mountains of the Alps divide Italy from its neighbors: France to the west, Switzerland and Austria to the north, and Yugoslavia to the east.

Italy has about 8,000 km (5,000 miles) of contrasting coastline. In some places it is hilly and rocky. Elsewhere, the beaches are long, flat and sandy. The coast plays an important part in Italy's economy, for as well as the many fine harbors and busy seaports, there are also a great number of popular seaside resorts that attract many tourists.

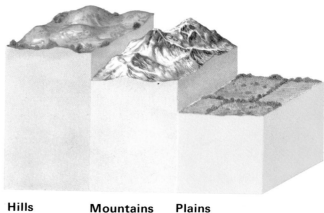

Hills
42%

Mountains
34%

Plains
24%

Above: Much of Italy is mountainous or hilly. Some of the mountains, such as Vesuvius, are volcanic. Lowland plains make up less than a quarter of the land area.

Below: Tuscany is a large region in north central Italy with a long history of settlement and cultivation. The region has many vineyards on the sunny slopes.

Above: Lake Orta in northern Italy.

Left: The high Alpine peaks near the Swiss border dwarf the ski-resort of Bormio.

Below: The varied landscape on Sicily includes these upland pastures near Enna, in the central region. Sicily is the largest island in the Mediterranean Sea.

Almost four-fifths of Italy is either mountainous or hilly. The Alps stretch for 1,300 km (800 miles) along Italy's northern borders, varying in width between 45 and 240 km (28 and 150 miles). On the frontier are some of the highest peaks, including Mont Blanc (4,807 m or 15,771 ft). In the foothills there are a number of large lakes. The Apennines extend for 1,200 km (750 miles) down the entire Italian peninsula.

Italy's main lowland regions are the broad, flat valley of the River Po and the Adriatic plain, both in the north, and the western coastal plain.

Situated off the "toe" of Italy is the rugged, triangular-shaped island of Sicily, where Mount Etna, Europe's highest volcano, rises to 3,340 m (10,958 ft). The island of Sardinia, to the northwest, is also mountainous.

Mainland Italy also contains two tiny independent states completely surrounded by Italian territory. One of these is the Republic of San Marino, which occupies 61 sq km (24 sq miles); the other is the Vatican City State, occupying just 0.44 sq km (0.17 sq miles).

The people

For thousands of years, Italy has attracted large numbers of foreign settlers. The earliest of these were the Etruscans, who lived mainly in Tuscany. The Greeks had colonies in southern Italy, and other early Italian people included the Phoenicians, Normans and Gauls.

The Romans, who are thought to have been descended from Germanic peoples, first settled in the Latium region in central Italy. Although they were successful, built impressive cities and ruled a large empire, at the time of Augustus (63 BC–AD 14) there were less than seven million people living in the area occupied by present-day Italy. After the collapse of the Empire, many of the cities were destroyed by invading barbarians and the native people were often forced to retreat to rather inhospitable regions. Over the following 12 centuries there were many other invasions by foreign nations as well as power struggles between and within the independent Italian states. Only in 1870 were the people of Italy united as one nation.

Above: The Roman Catholic Church has an important place in Italian life. These children are dressed up for their first communion.

Below: Many Italians enjoy sitting with friends in order to indulge in lively conversations or just to watch the rest of the world go by.

Above: Fabrizio Zavattaro, a farmer.

Above: Suor Amalia, a nun.

Below: Marco Ricagni, a flower seller.

Below: Stefano Ferreri, a businessman.

This complex history has resulted in the many individual dialects spoken by the Italian people, even within one region. Some of the border regions still have strong non-Italian influences in their language and culture. For example, many of the people of the Aosta Valley in the northwest of the country speak French as their first language, and there are Greek and Albanian-speaking families in Apulia.

Italian people are, in general, very jovial, warm and extrovert. They are also rather excitable and will discuss almost everything in a highly animated manner – from the everyday things of life (especially their health) to complex political matters. They communicate not only with words, but often also with expressions and gestures. Feelings and emotions are not held back, and that which to a foreigner might appear as a serious dispute is probably just a friendly and lively exchange of opinions. Like other Mediterranean people, Italians are not very fond of rigid discipline and do not like standing in line and waiting their turn.

Above: An Italian soldier.

Below: Giovanna Martini, a computer operator.

Where people live

More than 57 million people live in Italy, over half of them in cities and towns. The most densely populated parts of the country are the industrial triangle between Turin, Milan and Genoa in the north, and the coastal strip between Rome and Naples further south.

About a third of the Italian population live in the 48 cities with populations of more than 100,000 people. Rome, the capital and largest city, has just under three million inhabitants, while three other cities – Milan, Naples and Turin – have more than a million people. Genoa is the next largest city with a population of around 730,000 people.

Italy's long and important past is reflected in many of its towns and cities. Rome, for example, has been a major city for more than 2,000 years, and has been a capital of empire, state and republic. The city of Rome is also the site of the Vatican City State, the headquarters of the Roman Catholic Church.

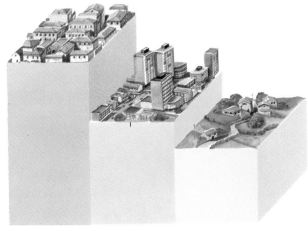

Towns
48%

Cities
30%

Rural areas
22%

Above: Only about a quarter of the Italian people live in rural areas. In recent years, however, some people have returned to the land.

Below: Murano, a suburb of Venice, is, like the rest of the city, built on a series of islands within the lagoon. Venice has been settled for about 1,500 years.

Many other Italian cities, too, including Naples, Venice, Florence, Bologna and Palermo, were the proud capitals of separate states in centuries past and are still of economic and cultural importance. Naples, for example, was once the capital of the former Kingdom of the Two Sicilies. Florence, as well as being a state capital, was a focus for the arts, especially during the Renaissance period.

During the 20th century, the growth of industry in northern Italy has been an important reason for the great increase in population there.

The greatest changes in the spread of population came after World War II. In order to find work, large numbers of people abandoned the country areas to live in the cities and towns. Over five million migrated from the rural south to the industrial north. Many left the mountainous regions, which were difficult to farm, to find work on the plains. Others moved to the coast, where many new towns, tourist resorts and industries were built on reclaimed marshlands.

Above: Palermo, the capital of Sicily, is a city of about 700,000 people. This ancient city is also an important port.

Below: A view of Sili, a village in the sparsely populated Calabria region which occupies the "toe" of Italy.

Rome

Rome, one of the world's most beautiful cities, was made the capital of Italy when the numerous separate states were united in 1870. But Rome has also been a major focus of European civilization for more than 2,000 years and has had an almost continuous influence on European government, religion and culture. For this reason Rome has become known as the "Eternal City."

Rome is situated on the River Tiber, about 25 km (16 miles) from the sea in central Italy. According to legend, the city was founded by Romulus in about 753 BC. Ancient Rome was built on seven hills situated on the left bank of the Tiber, but the city has since spread over the surrounding area and now covers about 210 sq km (81 sq miles), stretching almost to the sea. Today, Rome is a city of nearly three million people. It is divided into 22 central districts (or *rioni*); 18 residential boroughs (*quartieri*); and 11 outer suburbs (*suburbi*).

Above: The city of Rome still has many imposing columns, arches and other ruins which remain from the ancient Roman Empire.

Below: A plan of Rome showing some of the most famous buildings, streets and squares. The city was built at the lowest ford of the River Tiber.

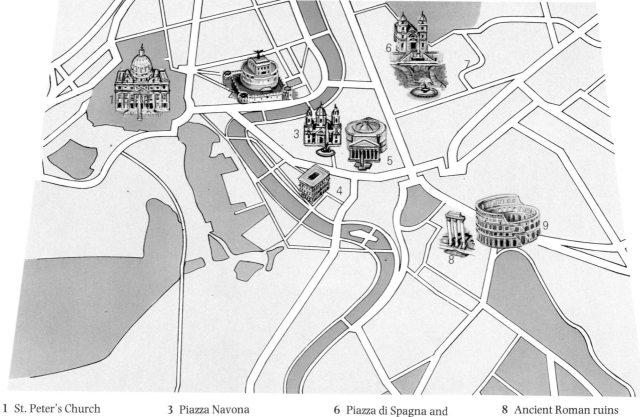

1 St. Peter's Church
2 Castel Sant' Angelo (a Medieval fortress)
3 Piazza Navona
4 Palazzo Farnese
5 The Pantheon
6 Piazza di Spagna and Spanish Steps
7 Via Vittorio Veneto
8 Ancient Roman ruins
9 The Colosseum

The ruins of ancient Roman buildings, including imperial palaces, temples, arches and public baths, can still be seen amid the bustle of the modern city. Among the most impressive are the almost intact Pantheon and the huge public entertainment arena known as the Colosseum.

Rome also contains many architectural masterpieces built in later centuries. Standing out among the many fine churches is the immense Basilica of St. Peter's, the heart of the world's Roman Catholic Church. There are also impressive government buildings, great palaces, such as the Farnese, and lovely squares, including the long Piazza Navona and the Piazza di Spagna, with its well-known Spanish Steps. Among the city's famous fountains is the popular Trevi Fountain, into which visitors traditionally throw coins to ensure their return.

Rome is also known for its beautiful public parks and elegant shopping streets, such as the Via Condotti and the Via Vittorio Veneto, which is also lined with smart hotels and cafes.

Above left: A view of Rome showing a mixture of old cathedrals and churches together with more recently built offices and apartments.

Above: The famous St. Peter's Church is visited by many tourists and pilgrims.
Below: A Papal audience in St. Peter's Square.

Fact file: land and population

Key facts

Location: Italy is a peninsula in southern Europe, which extends into the Mediterranean Sea. Italy is located between latitudes 36°40′ and 47° North and longitudes 6°40′ and 18°40′ East.

Main parts: Italy contains 20 regions, 18 of which are on the mainland. The two island regions are Sicily, area 25,708 sq km (9,926 sq miles), and Sardinia, area 24,090 sq km (9,301 sq miles). Smaller islands include the volcanic Lipari (or Aeolian) group off the north coast of Sicily, Ischia and Capri bordering the Bay of Naples, and Elba, which lies off the Tuscan coast in northwestern Italy.

Area: 301,225 sq km (116,304 sq miles).

Population: 57,317,000 (1987 estimate).

Capital city: Rome.

Major cities (with English and Italian names) and 1986 populations:

Rome (Roma, 2,815,000)
Milan (Milano, 1,495,000)
Naples (Napoli 1,204,000)
Turin (Torino, 1,036,000)
Genoa (Genova, 727,000)
Palermo (724,000)
Bologna (432,000)
Florence (Firenze, 426,000)
Catania (372,000)
Bari (363,000)
Venice (Venezia, 331,000)
Messina (269,000)
Verona (259,000)
Taranto (245,000)
Trieste (239,000)

Language: Italian is the official language. Each part of Italy has its own dialect. The Florentine dialect is the basis of modern Italian.

Highest point: Mont Blanc, in the Alps on Italy's border with France, is 4,807 m (15,771 ft) above sea-level. Italy's highest active volcano is Mount Etna, Sicily, at 3,340 m (10,958 ft).

Longest rivers: Po, 670 km (416 miles) and Tiber, 406 km (252 miles).

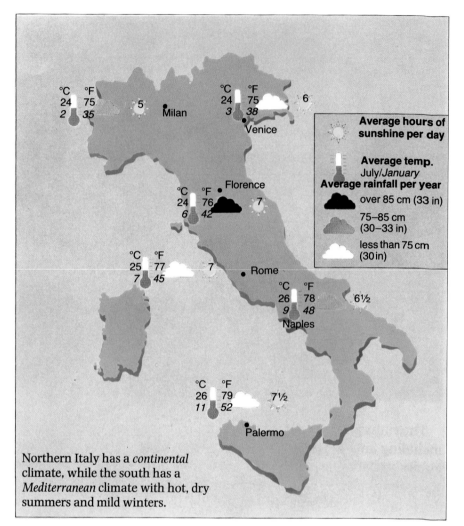

Northern Italy has a *continental* climate, while the south has a *Mediterranean* climate with hot, dry summers and mild winters.

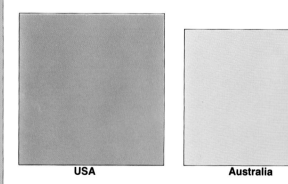

△ **A land area comparison**
Italy has an area of 301,225 sq km (116,304 sq miles). This is only about 1/30th the size of the United States (9,370,000 sq km, 3,600,000 sq miles) and is also much less than the area of Australia (7,650,000 sq km, 2,470,000 sq miles). Italy is bigger than the United Kingdom which has an area of 244,030 sq km (94,220 sq miles).

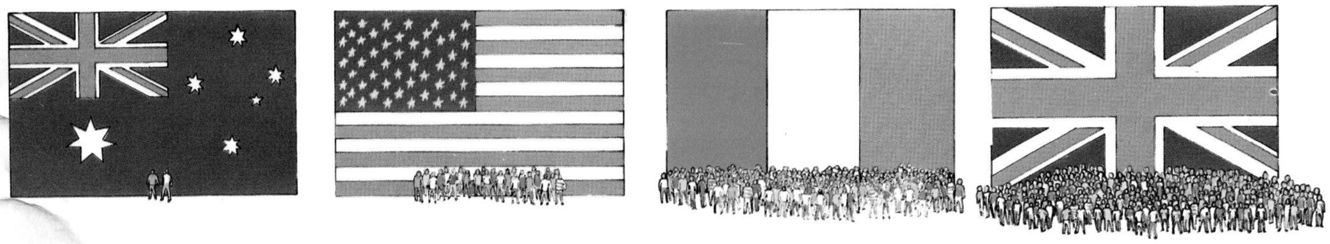

Australia 2 per sq km

USA 25 per sq km

Italy 190 per sq km

UK 229 per sq km

△ **A population density comparison**
Italy has a fairly high population
density in world terms and has the
fifth highest density in Europe.

Trieste

Milan

Venice

Verona

Turin

Genoa

Bologna

Leghorn

Florence

Rome

Bari

Naples

Brindisi

Taranto

Major cities

Main ports

Main routeways

Messina

▷ **Italy's major cities, ports and
routeways**
The majority of Italian cities are in
the busy north, although the large
cities of Rome, Naples and Palermo
are located further south.

Palermo

Catania

Augusta

Home life

Family life is important to Italians and they like to keep in close and regular contact with all their relatives. They take great pride in their homes, which are always kept neat, clean and attractive.

A typical Italian family living in a town has a two- or three-bedroomed apartment, sometimes with garage space. People living in the suburbs often own attractive modern houses with well-planted gardens.

Some homes only have a small kitchen, next to which is a medium-sized room called the *tinello*, where the family takes its meals. This is also the most lived-in room in the home and the place where the family usually gathers. The children often play or do their homework here, and visitors dropping in for a chat sit around the big central table.

The living room, or *salotto*, is used for more formal entertaining. It usually contains the television and the best furniture, with cabinets displaying china, silver or glass.

Above: The Bianchi family of Turin, outside their home. Most older apartment houses are only four to six stories high.

Left: The Bianchi family relax in their living room. Gabriella Bianchi is reading *La Stampa*, a popular Turin newspaper.

When they are not watching television, Italian families sometimes amuse themselves by playing cards, dominoes, chess or other games. At the end of the year it is traditional to play *tombola*, or bingo, with friends and to give small presents to the winners.

Italians love social gatherings and often entertain relatives and friends at home. Guests may be invited just for evening coffee, when they may eat special sweets or pastries as they chat. People invited for lunch or dinner, however, are treated to a more elaborate meal, which may include some of the hostess's special recipes.

Sleeping space in Italian homes is sometimes limited, and the children, especially the younger ones, may have to share bedrooms and perhaps sleep in bunk beds. Storage space in the small flats or apartments is also limited, but there is often extra space on the balcony, while houses may have a cellar, or *cantina*. The most modern homes also contain a utility room which again provides extra storage space.

Shops and shopping

Supermarkets are not common in Italy, so housewives generally do their household shopping in the small shops and in the local market. Most Italian towns and villages have markets. They are always bustling with people and packed with bright and colorful stalls that sell all kinds of fresh foods and many other items besides.

Food can also be bought in the many different kinds of small shops. There are bakeries, shops that sell milk and cheese, butchers, fishmarkets, general grocers, fruit and vegetable stores and many more. Some are even more highly specialized, such as those butchers' shops that sell only veal or pork.

In small or remote country or mountain villages there is often only one general store that sells almost everything that people need for everyday life. Tobacco stores in Italy have a special government license and also sell postage stamps, salt, legal documents and special stamps for renewing passports and driving licenses.

Above: Fruit and vegetable stalls in the market at Lecco in Lombardy sell both local fruit such as grapefruit and imported produce like pineapples.

Below: A hardware store and other small shops and stalls at Pozzuoli, near the city of Naples. These cater for the needs of both the local residents and tourists.

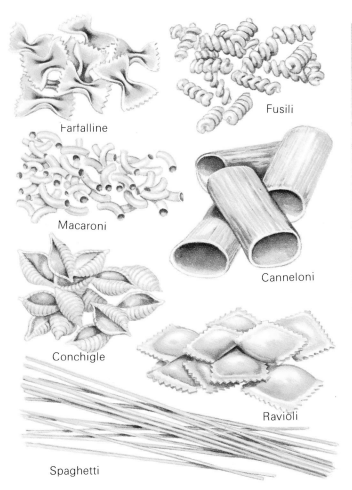

Farfalline

Fusili

Macaroni

Canneloni

Conchigle

Ravioli

Spaghetti

Italy's few supermarkets are mainly found in the cities and towns. There are also a number of large hypermarkets on the outskirts of some towns, where shoppers can buy goods in bulk at discount prices.

In the middle of every Italian city and town there is always a main shopping street where the most fashionable and elegant shops are found. Here shoppers can buy articles such as clothes, shoes, linen, leather goods and gifts. Some of Italy's most famous shopping streets are the Via Condotti in Rome, the Via Montenapoleone in Milan, the Via Roma in Turin, the Via Tornabuoni in Florence, and the streets in the vicinity of St. Mark's Square in Venice.

Italian shops are generally open every day except Sunday between 8.30 a.m. and 7.30 p.m., but close for lunch from 1.00 p.m. to 3.30 p.m. They also remain closed one afternoon during the week, the day varying from town to town.

Above left: Some of the types of pasta sold in Italy. Hundreds of different varieties are available. Pasta has been made since ancient times.

Above: A supermarket near Chiasso in northern Italy.
Below: A typical Italian shopping basket would include olive oil and pasta.

Cooking and eating

Italians enjoy the good things in life – especially fine food, whether at home or in restaurants. They also like to drink good wine, which in Italy is both plentiful and cheap. Italian food is famous for its great variety and its rich flavor. Housewives spend a lot of time preparing food from basic ingredients and rarely use packaged or pre-cooked meals.

Every region of Italy has its own special dishes, and there are many differences in cooking and eating habits between the north and south of the country. Generally, breakfast consists only of coffee and a roll. Lunch, at midday, is the main meal of the day, while dinner is usually lighter.

Pizza and pasta are two Italian dishes that are well known throughout the world. Pizza, originally from Naples, consists of a doughy base with various toppings, usually including cheese. Other ingredients in the topping may include olives, anchovies, mushrooms, tomatoes, peppers and capers.

Above: Gabriella and Stefania Bianchi prepare a spaghetti dish in their modern kitchen.

Left: The Bianchi family eat a simple meal of cold meats and bread. Wine is served with most meals.

Below: A mixed pasta dish, such as the one shown here, is often served as the first course of a meal.

Pasta is made in all kinds of shapes and is served with many different sauces. It is usually eaten as the first course of a meal, followed by a main course of meat and vegetables or salad, then cheese, and finally fruit or a dessert. Wine and mineral water are drunk with the meal, followed by coffee.

Italians often have their Sunday lunch in a restaurant. Families and friends may also dine together in a restaurant on Christmas Day and at Easter. At these times, and during other important festivals throughout the year, special traditional dishes are eaten.

Eel, grilled or cooked in tomato sauce, is traditionally eaten on Christmas Eve. On Christmas Day people sit down to a huge and elaborate meal consisting of many starters, stuffed pasta, roast meat (generally turkey or veal) with vegetables, and cheese. The traditional light Christmas cake, or *panettone*, is served at the end. At Easter, it is the custom to eat roast lamb and a dove-shaped cake filled with almonds and candied peel.

Pastimes and sports

Every year about four out of every ten Italians go away from home for their vacation, although only a comparatively small number venture abroad. During the summer months most go to the many crowded and lively seaside resorts scattered along Italy's long coastline. Others prefer the peace and quiet of the mountains or the countryside.

Many Italian families now own second homes in these areas as an escape from the pressures of modern city life. Here they can enjoy all kinds of outdoor leisure activities including swimming, sailing, walking, mountaineering and skiing.

Skiing is a particularly popular sport in Italy, and the ski slopes in the Alps and Apennines are crowded from December to May. At the highest resorts in the Aosta Valley and the Dolomites it is possible to ski even during the height of summer.

Left: Most major soccer matches in Italy are played on Sunday afternoons.
Below: A colorful stall offers a variety of soccer souvenirs.

Above: Sestri Levante is a popular seaside resort near Genoa. Most Italians spend their vacations at Italian resorts rather than going abroad.

Italians also enjoy tennis, fencing, horse riding, hunting, fishing and many other leisure activities. But the most popular sport of all is soccer, and children can be seen playing it everywhere. Italians are keen soccer fans, and every Sunday the stadiums in big towns are crowded with noisy supporters attending games and waving the colorful flags of their teams. Among the most famous professional teams in Italy are *Juventus, Torino, Milano, Inter* and *Roma.*

Another popular sporting event is the *Giro d'Italia* bicycle race held every spring. Everyone turns out to watch the riders pass as they criss-cross the entire length of the country during the three-week competition. Because so much of Italy is mountainous, Italian cyclists are second only to the Spanish as the world's best "climbers."

Also held in Italy is the famous *Mille Miglia*, a 1,000-mile (1,600-km) motor race that is one of the most demanding contests held on open roads in the world. Motor races on the spectacular track at Monza, in northern Italy, also attract large crowds.

Above: Strolling in the park is a pastime enjoyed by many Italian families. Crowds gather in this park in Turin on most Sundays throughout the year.

Below: Cycling provides enjoyable exercise for all the family. The Bianchis will probably head for the country away from the pollution of the town.

News and entertainment

There are seven nationally available Italian newspapers, of which the one with the largest circulation is *Il Corriere della Sera*, published in Milan. Other popular newspapers are *La Stampa*, published in Turin, and *Il Giornale*, published in Rome.

Specialist newspapers are also available, such as those covering sport and business. There are also many regional and local newspapers. In addition, the Italians have a choice of over 3,000 weekly and monthly magazines published in their country as well as the more popular foreign magazines.

In Italy, as in many other countries, watching television is a popular leisure activity. Over 90 per cent of Italian households have at least one television and one in three of these is a color television.

Above: A street newsstand. Around five million newspapers are bought each day in Italy.

Below: Some popular Italian magazines. *Grazia* is a weekly women's magazine. *Oggi* is also published weekly and contains illustrated articles on topical issues.

Above: Italian children, like young people all over the world, enjoy reading pop magazines and cartoon strips.

Italy has three state-controlled channels: RAI1, RAI2 and RAI3. There are also over a hundred independent television channels, four of which have national coverage. In some areas of the country it is possible to pick up about 24 different stations. The state channels begin broadcasting in the late morning, and finish for the day at about 11 or 11.30 p.m. Most of the independent stations broadcast for longer, usually starting at about 8 a.m. and finishing at 1 or 2 a.m. the following day. Some provide 24-hour transmissions.

Televised sport, films, soap operas and quizzes are all popular in Italy. Some of the highest viewing figures have been recorded for sports: over 32 million people (more than half the Italian population) have watched some recent sports programs. A viewing figure of about 15 million is more normal for most popular programs, however.

Foreign television is also available in some of the regions; for example TV Svizzera (from Switzerland) is broadcast in some of the northern regions, such as Piedmont and Lombardy.

Above left: Newspapers such as *Stampa Sera* and *La Notte* are on sale throughout Italy. Many local papers are also available.

Above: A sunny street cafe is the ideal place to read the newspaper while relaxing over a drink.

Below: An Italian television guide.

Fact file: home life and leisure

Key facts

Population composition: People under 15 years of age make up 22 per cent of the population, people between 15 and 64 make up 64.6 per cent, and people 65 and over make up 13.4 per cent.

Average life expectancy at birth: 76 years (1983), as compared with 72 in 1970. (In the USA, people live, on average, 75 years, but in India, the average life expectancy is only 55 years.) Women make up 51.2 per cent of Italy's population. The average life expectancy of women is 79 years, 6 years more than men.

Rate of population increase: 0.4 per cent a year between 1970 and 1982, as compared with 0.7 per cent a year between 1960 and 1970. The falling rate of population increase is in line with most Western countries.

Family life: *Number of marriages (1983): 300,855; Number of divorces (1984): 15,030.*

Homes: In 1979, 41 per cent of Italian homes were rented and 59 per cent were owner-occupied.

Work: The average working week in Italy is about 40 hours. The total workforce in April 1982 was 22 million, of which 8.6 per cent were unemployed.

Prices: Prices rose by 3.6 per cent per year between 1960 and 1970 and by 13.1 per cent a year between 1970 and 1982. In 1982/83 the rate of inflation had reached 14.6 per cent.

Religions: More than 95 per cent of Italians are Roman Catholics and the government of the Roman Catholic Church, headed by the Pope, is in the Vatican City, a tiny but independent state entirely within the city of Rome. There are also some Protestants and about 50,000 Jews.

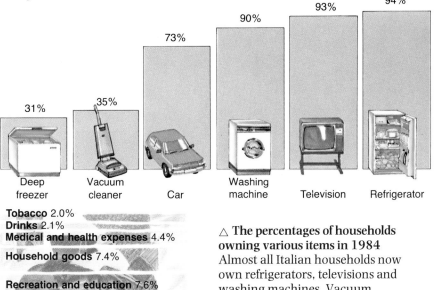

31% Deep freezer
35% Vacuum cleaner
73% Car
90% Washing machine
93% Television
94% Refrigerator

Tobacco 2.0%
Drinks 2.1%
Medical and health expenses 4.4%
Household goods 7.4%
Recreation and education 7.6%
Clothing and footwear 9.0%
Transport and communications 13.5%
Rent, fuel and power 13.5%
Other goods and services 15.3%
Food 25.2%

△ **The percentages of households owning various items in 1984**
Almost all Italian households now own refrigerators, televisions and washing machines. Vacuum cleaners are not very common in Italy, because floors are often tiled rather than covered with carpet.

◁ **How the average household budget was spent in 1984**
The Italians now spend less of their budget on food, drink and tobacco than they did in the 1970s.

▽ **Italian currency and stamps**
The unit of Italian currency is the lira (plural lire). Coins are issued for values between 5 and 500 lire and notes for between 500 and 100,00 lire. In 1986 there were about 1,625 lire to the US dollar.

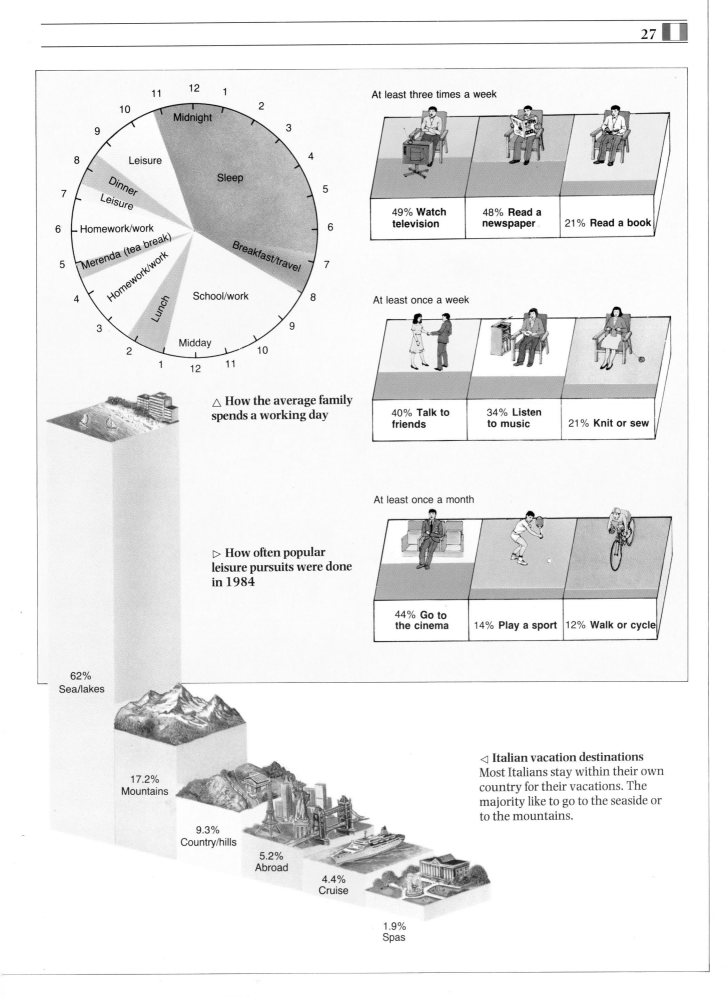

△ **How the average family spends a working day**

At least three times a week

| 49% **Watch television** | 48% **Read a newspaper** | 21% **Read a book** |

At least once a week

| 40% **Talk to friends** | 34% **Listen to music** | 21% **Knit or sew** |

▷ **How often popular leisure pursuits were done in 1984**

At least once a month

| 44% **Go to the cinema** | 14% **Play a sport** | 12% **Walk or cycle** |

62% Sea/lakes

17.2% Mountains

9.3% Country/hills

5.2% Abroad

4.4% Cruise

1.9% Spas

◁ **Italian vacation destinations**
Most Italians stay within their own country for their vacations. The majority like to go to the seaside or to the mountains.

Farming and fishing

About four-fifths of the land in Italy is not ideally suited to crop farming, because it is mountainous or hilly. Despite this, agriculture is an important part of the Italian economy. There are over three million farms in the country, most of which are worked by the owner and his family. They average about 7 hectares (17 acres) in area, with larger farms in the mountainous areas and smaller ones in the lowlands.

Nearly half of the farms in Italy specialize in the cultivation of vines and they produce over 21 per cent of the world's wine. Among the best-known exported varieties of wine are Barolo, Soave, Chianti, Valpolicella, Frascati and Marsala.

Italy is the world's second largest producer of olive oil, which comes mainly from the southern regions of Apulia, Calabria and Sicily. The south is also famous for citrus fruits, including oranges, tangerines, lemons and limes.

Above: A Tuscan farming family all help with the pruning at the end of the season. Most Italians farms are family owned and run.

Below: Soil being dug over in a vineyard in Apulia. The scattered dwellings, known as *trulli*, are typical of this region.

Above: Plowing the fertile red soils of the Po Valley in northern Italy.

Left: Some Italian cheeses.

Below: Oysters, octopus, red mullet, whiting and sardines are among the seafood caught off the Italian coast.

Vegetables, too, are widely cultivated throughout the south and in Sardinia. The main crops are tomatoes, potatoes, artichokes, garlic, onions, cauliflowers and beans. Tobacco is another important crop in the south, while sugar beet is produced in great quantities on northern farms. The cultivation of flowers is of increasing importance in the Italian economy, and the flowers are exported as well as sold in Italy.

The main Italian cereal crops are wheat, for making bread and pasta, and corn (maize). Italy is also an important producer of rice, which is grown in the fertile Po Valley areas of Piedmont and Lombardy in the north.

Large numbers of animals are raised on Italian farms, including pigs, cattle, sheep, goats, horses and poultry. Dairy farms are found throughout the country, but the largest numbers are concentrated in Emilia-Romagna. This northern region produces the famous Parmesan cheese, one of Italy's many excellent types of cheese.

Natural resources and industry

Italy is not rich in metallic minerals, but iron ore is found in some of the older rocks in the Aosta Valley and in Sardinia, and quantities of lead, zinc and aluminum ores occur in the Alps, Tuscany, the Marches and Apulia. However, mercury ores are abundant, especially in Tuscany, and Italy is one of the world's main producers of this metal.

Salt and sulphur are mined in Sicily, and various types of Italian rock are used as building stones. The marble produced from the quarries at Carrara in Tuscany is world famous. Italy also has some coal and oil deposits, but most other raw materials and fuels have to be imported.

Because of the need to import materials, many of Italy's industries are based in coastal regions near the main ports. Milan and Turin are also important industrial centers and both these cities are served by major rail and road networks.

Above: Marble is quarried at Carrara. Marble from this area was used by the famous Italian sculptor Michelangelo.

Below: The large Italsider steelworks now dominate the old seaport of Piombino in Tuscany in north central Italy.

MOTO GUZZI

Above: The badges of some famous Italian car and motorcycle manufacturers.

Left: As it passes along the production line a Fiat Uno car body is dipped to protect it from rust.

Below: Domestic appliances are manufactured at the Zanussi factory near Venice.

Italian industrial production has expanded rapidly this century, and has tripled since World War II. Annual steel production has risen from virtually zero at the beginning of the century to 23 million tons, making Italy the fourth most important producer in Europe.

Large quantities of steel are needed for car manufacture, which is one of Italy's most important industries. Fiat, based in Turin, employs more than 200,000 people and produces almost one and a half million cars each year. Other well-known Italian car firms include Alfa Romeo, Ferrari, Maserati, Lamborghini and Iso. Many of the cars are prestigious and expensive models for export.

Italy's electrical industries also produce many goods for export. Domestic appliances are made by firms such as Zanussi, and 35,000 people are employed by around 135 firms in this type of industry.

Italy's chemical industry is an important producer of ammonia, synthetic resins, plastics, dyes and fertilizers. The country also has a flourishing pharmaceutical industry.

Fashion and design

The fashion and clothing trade is Italy's second largest industry, after tourism. Its products are admired world-wide, and foreign buyers pack the twice-yearly Milan *Collezione* (Collections), where some 30 fashion shows are staged. Together with Milan, Florence and Rome are the main centers of the clothing and fashion industry in Italy.

The success of the Italian fashion industry is not surprising, for Italian design has been renowned for centuries. Textiles have long been prized, and Italian silks, which are produced today by such firms as Ratti, have earned especial fame.

Italian fashion has an elegance all of its own. Brilliant color and *linea* (style) are evident in designs by famous fashion houses such as Biagiotti, Ungaro, Armani and Missoni. Gucci gives similar flair to Italian shoes and handbags. Italian clothes and other fashion items are often "signed" by designers or manufacturers, and this tends to make them exclusive and expensive.

Left: Gucci designs and makes some of the world's most exclusive shoes and handbags. The Gucci symbol is often part of the design.

Above: A model displays clothes designed by Biagiotti.
Below: Benetton clothes are popular for their chic designs and bright colors.

However, not all Italian fashion is costly. The famous fashion house, Benetton, which was founded in 1965, mass-produces knitwear which is not too expensive, and is warm, bright and well designed.

A similar excellence is achieved by Italian motor cars, furniture and lighting, domestic appliances, glass and jewelry. Designers are consulted throughout the development and manufacture of the items. Good design is considered to be just as important as practicality, and is not reserved just for the expensive end of the market. Even ordinary, everyday Italian cars, such as Fiats, are almost as pleasing to look at as the rather more expensive Ferraris.

Italian furniture design has been particularly influential. *Linea* is evident in items such as lamps, tables, stools and chairs. Simple, but eye-catching elegance marks the plastic and metal "space age" chairs which Italian designers have pioneered.

Above: This Ferrari car clearly shows the Italian flair for design.

Below: This modern Italian lamp has a striking and unusual design.

Transportation

Italians love motor cars, and they get a lot of pleasure from driving. For most people in Italy the car is the main means of transportation and most families have at least one car.

Because cars are so important, the Italian government has spent large sums building motorways, or *autostrade*. Drivers have to pay tolls as they pass along them. In the 1920s Italy became one of the the first European countries to build these fast highways and it now has a network of nearly 6,000 km (4,000 miles). It is the world's third largest system after those of the United States and West Germany. The most famous Italian motorway is the *Autostrada del Sole*. This recently completed road runs the length of the country from Milan to Reggio in Calabria.

Italy's railroad network did not extend throughout the whole country until the 20th century. Today, there are 19,782 km (12,292 miles) of track, which is used mainly for passenger transport. There are various kinds of trains, from the fast, long-distance *espresso* and *rapido*, to the local *accellerato*.

Above: An *autostrada* tollgate. The charges made depend on the size of the vehicle and the distance traveled along the *autostrada* network.

Below: An electric train in Piedmont. Despite the Italian love of cars, many people use public transportation to get to work each day.

Above: The symbols used by the state airline and railway companies.

Left: A passenger ferry crosses scenic Lake Maggiore in Lombardy, northern Italy.

Below: Genoa is Italy's chief seaport, and exports include olive oil, wine and textiles. Many foreign ships use the port.

Air transport in Italy, both for passengers and freight, has expanded greatly in recent years. Almost all major cities have their own airport, while Rome and Milan each have two. The airports at Rimini and Venice are the next most important, because they handle large numbers of tourists. Italy's national airline, Alitalia, carries over seven million passengers a year worldwide.

Compared with France, West Germany and the Netherlands, Italy's network of inland waterways is small. However, the River Po is navigable for much of its length and is used for transporting freight to such cities as Mantua and Cremona. Ferryboats are important for transportation on the great northern lakes.

Italy's long coastline is dotted with many seaports, which are used by both passenger liners and merchant ships. The most important are Genoa, Trieste, Venice, Naples, Leghorn and La Spezia.

Fact file: economy and trade

◁ **The distribution of economic activity in Italy**
The Po Valley, running across northern Italy, is the most important agricultural region in the country. Industry is also concentrated in the north of the country and along the western coast around Rome and Naples.

	Industry
	Petroleum
	Cattle
	Sheep
	Wheat
	Rice
	Grapes
	Olives
	Fishing
	Mulberry leaves (for silk)
	Citrus fruits

Key facts

Structure of production: Of the total GDP (the value of all economic activity in Italy), farming, forestry and fishing contribute 5 per cent, industry 39 per cent, and services 56 per cent.
Farming: *Main products:* barley, fruit, wine, maize, olives, rice, sugar beet, tobacco, vegetables, wheat, *Livestock:* cattle 8,921,000; sheep and goats, 12,652,000; pigs, 9,278,000.

Fishing: The catch in 1985 was nearly 430,000 tonnes
Mining: Italy ranks seventh in western Europe in producing oil. It is self-sufficient only in mercury and sulphur.
Energy: Of the total electrical energy produced in 1984, power stations using coal, gas or oil contributed 76 per cent, hydroelectric stations 32 per cent and nuclear power stations 2 per cent.

Manufacturing: Italy produces textiles, footwear, food, tobacco, engineering products, farm and industrial machinery, iron and steel, and chemicals.
Trade (1986): *Total imports:* US $98,000 million; *Exports:* US $96,431 million.
Economic growth: The average growth rate of Italy's gross national product between 1980 and 1987 was 1.3 per cent per year.

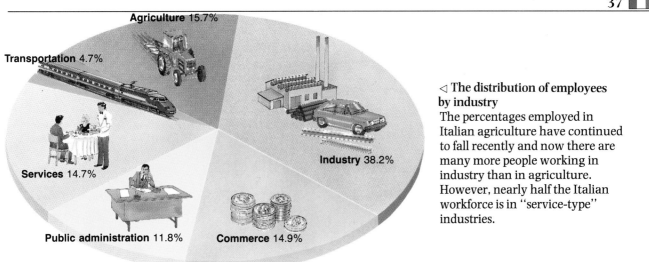

Agriculture 15.7%

Transportation 4.7%

Services 14.7%

Public administration 11.8%

Commerce 14.9%

Industry 38.2%

◁ **The distribution of employees by industry**
The percentages employed in Italian agriculture have continued to fall recently and now there are many more people working in industry than in agriculture. However, nearly half the Italian workforce is in "service-type" industries.

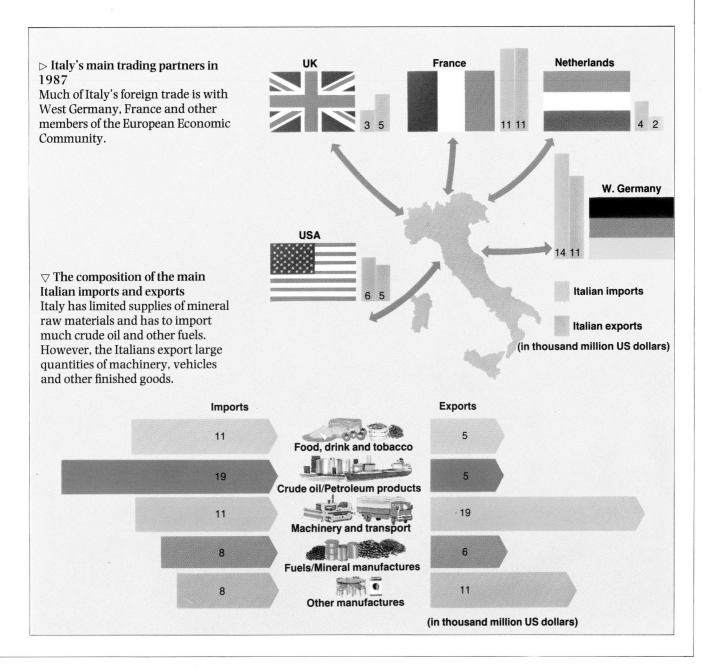

▷ **Italy's main trading partners in 1987**
Much of Italy's foreign trade is with West Germany, France and other members of the European Economic Community.

UK
3 5

France
11 11

Netherlands
4 2

W. Germany
14 11

USA
6 5

Italian imports

Italian exports

(in thousand million US dollars)

▽ **The composition of the main Italian imports and exports**
Italy has limited supplies of mineral raw materials and has to import much crude oil and other fuels. However, the Italians export large quantities of machinery, vehicles and other finished goods.

Imports		Exports
11	Food, drink and tobacco	5
19	Crude oil/Petroleum products	5
11	Machinery and transport	19
8	Fuels/Mineral manufactures	6
8	Other manufactures	11

(in thousand million US dollars)

Education

All Italian children between the ages of 6 and 14 must attend school. Most schools are provided and run by the government, but there are also private schools.

Some Italian parents send their children to kindergarten or nursery school before they are six. But most children begin their education at a primary school, or *Scuola Elementare*. After five years, at the age of 11, they move on to a junior secondary school, or *Scuola Media Inferiore*, for three years. These schools help the children to decide what kind of studies they are best suited to when they go on to a senior secondary school, or *Scuola Media Superiore*, at the age of 14.

Many choose to attend a *Liceo*, which offers an academic type of education specializing in Ancient Greek and Latin studies, the arts, languages, or sciences. Others prefer to go to a technical institute, which provides courses more closely linked to possible future employment in commerce, industry or agriculture. Some students decide to take courses at a teacher-training college.

Above: Children play outside their primary school in Turin. Classes are limited to 20 pupils.

Left: A class at a primary school. There are over 26,000 government-run primary schools in Italy.

At the end of their five-year courses, students take the nationwide examination (*Esame di Stato*) for a diploma that will qualify them for a place at an Italian university. The government provides financial help to both Italian and foreign students who wish to attend Italian universities.

Italy has 59 universities in 36 cities. The oldest, Bologna, was founded in 1135, while the largest is in Rome. Other famous Italian universities include Pisa, Padua, Pavia, Milan and Naples. At the end of their courses, which last for between four and six years, successful students receive their *laurea*, or degree. Students who obtain good degrees may then go on to do research.

Professional training in music, fine arts, drama and dance in Italy is provided by a number of famous academies. There is also a well-known film training school in Rome, the center of the Italian film industry.

Above: The school uniform worn by these girls is typical of that worn at many Italian government-run schools.

Below: Teenagers at a school in Rome attend an English lesson. All Italians have to study a foreign language at school.

The arts

Few countries can match the impressive achievements of Italy in the arts. Over many centuries Italians have created masterpieces, not only in painting, sculpture and architecture, but also in literature, music and the cinema.

Most of the world's great museums contain sculptures and other works of art created by artists of the great Roman civilization that existed some 2,000 years ago. Relics of Roman temples, theaters, baths and other buildings can still be seen in Rome and other parts of the former empire.

During the 15th and 16th centuries a period of great activity in all the arts, known as the Renaissance, began in Italy. Among the best-known artists of this time were Leonardo da Vinci (1452–1519), whose paintings include the famous portrait known as the *Mona Lisa*, and Michelangelo (1475–1564), whose work included a huge statue of David and paintings inside the Sistine Chapel in the Vatican, Rome. Two other outstanding artists of the Renaissance were the painters Raphael (1483–1520) and Titian (*c.* 1487–1576).

Above: Sandro Botticelli's painting *Mystic Nativity*, which was completed in 1500, is an example of early Italian Renaissance art.

Left: The beautiful city of Florence houses many of Italy's finest works of art. It also has numerous buildings of great architectural merit, such as the cathedral seen here.

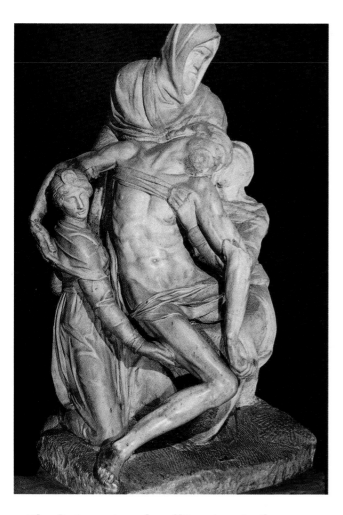

Left: Michelangelo's sculpture *Pietà*.
Below: The famous Italian poet Dante Alighieri (1265–1321).

Above: A scene from Giuseppe Verdi's opera *Falstaff*, which was first performed in Milan in 1893.

The first great works of literature in the Italian language were written in about 1300 by the poet Dante Alighieri, the author of *The Divine Comedy*. Other early writers were the poet and scholar Francesco Petrarca (or Petrarch, 1304–74) and the story-teller Giovanni Boccaccio (1313–75), who wrote a book of witty tales known as the *Decameron*. Later writers include the novelist Alessandro Manzoni (1785–1873) and the playwright Luigi Pirandello (1867–1936).

Italy has also produced many outstanding musicians, both composers and singers. Opera houses around the world still perform the works of Gioacchino Rossini (1792–1868), Giuseppe Verdi (1813–1901), Giacomo Puccini (1858–1924) and other great composers.

The cinema is another popular art form in Italy, and directors such as Roberto Rossellini (1906–77), Luchino Visconti (1906–76) and Federico Fellini (1920–) have created many fine films.

The making of modern Italy

In the 5th century AD, the once-mighty Roman Empire began to crumble in western Europe as German invaders swept into and conquered the Italian peninsula, including Rome itself. For centuries afterwards, Italy remained divided into small, separate states ruled either by the Pope or by foreign powers such as Germany, France, Spain or Austria.

A struggle for freedom from Austrian rule and for the unification of all the separate Italian states began in the 19th century. It was led by the revolutionary Giuseppe Mazzini, the warrior Giuseppe Garibaldi, and the statesman Count Camillo di Cavour.

After some successes Victor Emmanuel II of Sardinia was proclaimed King of Italy in 1861. But the country was not finally united until 1870 with the capture of Rome and the Papal States.

During World War I Italy fought on the side of the Allies and in 1918 won important battles on its northeastern borders. As a result, Italy gained further territories in this region, including the town of Trieste.

Above: The Italian patriot Giuseppe Garibaldi helped to unite the many separate states of Italy in the mid-nineteenth century.

Below: Italian troops hauling a heavy gun through the pass at Isonzo, in present-day Yugoslavia, during World War I.

During the difficult years of recovery after the war, Benito Mussolini, the leader of a national group called Fascists, seized control of the government. By 1925 he had become the dictator of Italy. Under his rule Italy re-armed, occupied Ethiopia and Albania and, in 1940, entered World War II on Germany's side. However, in 1943 Italy changed sides and the Italians fought with the Allied Forces during the last 18 months of the war. In April 1945 Mussolini was killed by resistance fighters while trying to escape to Switzerland.

After the war, the Italian people held a referendum to vote on whether they wanted their country to be a monarchy or a republic. Nearly 13 million voted for a republic, compared with nearly 11 million for a monarchy. King Umberto II, who had only become king a month earlier, left the country, and at a meeting in Rome Enrico de Nicola was elected as the provisional head of state. A new constitution was drawn up, and came into force at the beginning of 1948.

Above left: Mussolini (right) in the 1920s.
Below: The monastery at Monte Cassino was left in ruins after the famous battle there in 1943.

Above: Many Italians opposed Fascism during World War II. Resistance fighters, known as Partisans, included many women.

Italy in the modern world

After World War II, the Italians had to rebuild their country, which had been devastated by two years of heavy fighting on its soil. Aided by an American-funded European Recovery Programme, the Italians also tackled their widespread unemployment and started on long-overdue land reforms and other plans to improve the poor agricultural regions of southern Italy.

Advances were also made in setting up new manufacturing and agricultural industries. By the 1960s, when Italy had signed the Treaty of Rome and become one of the founder members of the European Economic Community, the country was enjoying something of an industrial boom.

Since the abolition of the monarchy in 1946, Italy has suffered much political instability. The Italian presidents hold office for seven years, and thus provide some continuity, but no less than 26 separate governments had been formed under 12 prime ministers in the 30 years up to 1976.

Below left: In 1977, about 100,000 metal workers from all over Italy demonstrated in Rome against the government's economic policy.

Above: Signing the Treaty of Rome in 1957.

Below: Sandro Pertini was a popular recent president of Italy.

Left: Policing is a job now open to Italian women.

Below: Italy's high level of youth unemployment means poor job prospects for many young Italians.

Above: Italian agriculture has been modernized in recent years. This farmer uses a computer to help him control conditions for his chickens.

The effects of political instability were made even worse after 1973, when a sharp rise in the price of oil resulted in recession, unemployment and a series of financial crises.

By 1980 Italy faced many severe problems. The economy was in difficulties and there were violent protests against the government, political scandals and terrorist atrocities. One terrorist group kidnapped and murdered former Prime Minister Aldo Moro in 1978. Another bombed Bologna Railway Station in 1980, killing 85 people.

However, other aspects of Italy's post-war history are more positive. Life expectancy has risen since the war by ten or twelve years. Infant mortality has fallen from 10 to 2 per cent of live births in the last 40 years. Italians, and especially Italian women, now enjoy more personal freedom. Divorce has been legal since 1970 – despite church opposition – and husbands and wives now have equal rights over property and their children.

Fact file: government and world role

Aosta Valley

Trentino – Alto Adige

Friuli-Venezia Giulia

Lombardy (Lombardia)

Veneto

Piedmont (Piemonte)

Emilia – Romagna

Liguria

San Marino

The Marches (Marche)

Tuscany (Toscana)

Umbria

Abruzzi

Latium (Lazio)

Molise

Apulia (Puglia)

Campania

Basilicata

Sardinia (Sardegna)

Calabria

Sicily (Sicilia)

◁ **The regions of Italy**
Italy's 20 regions must abide by the laws which govern the country as a whole. but within these guidelines they are able to make many of their own local laws.

Key facts

Official name: *Repubblica Italiana* (Italian Republic).
Flag: Three vertical stripes of green, white and red.
National anthem: *Fratelli d'Italia*.
National government: *Head of State*: The President. The President appoints the Prime Minister, who is a member of the Chamber of Deputies. *Parliament*: Parliament consists of the directly elected Chamber of Deputies, with 630 members, and the Senate, whose 315 members are elected on a regional basis. Members of both houses are elected for five-year terms.
Local government: Italy contains 20 regions, which are further divided into provinces and municipalities (*comuni*). Each region, province and municipality has an elected council, called a *consiglio*, and an executive, called a *giunta*.

Armed forces: *Army*: The strength of the Army in 1985 was 260,000. *Air Force*: The Air Force had 70,600 personnel in 1983. *Navy*: 42,200 personnel (1985). There is compulsory military service for 12 months in the Army and Air Force, and 18 months in the Navy.
Political alliances: Italy belongs to the UN and the Council of Europe. It was a founder member of the North Atlantic Treaty Organization.

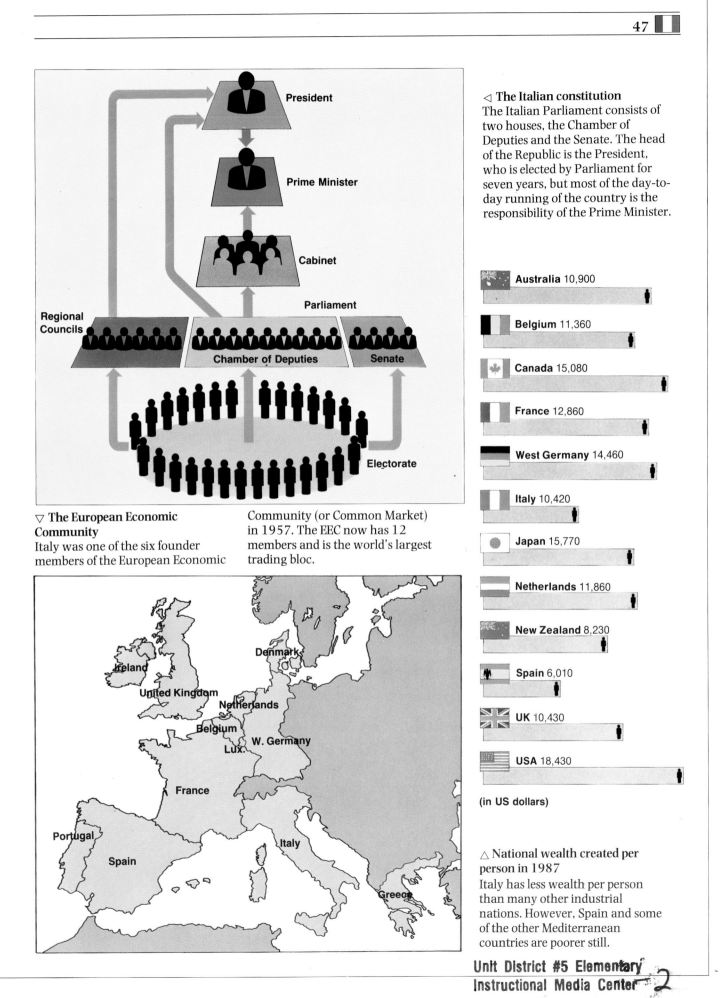

◁ **The Italian constitution**
The Italian Parliament consists of two houses, the Chamber of Deputies and the Senate. The head of the Republic is the President, who is elected by Parliament for seven years, but most of the day-to-day running of the country is the responsibility of the Prime Minister.

President

Prime Minister

Cabinet

Parliament

Regional Councils

Chamber of Deputies

Senate

Electorate

▽ **The European Economic Community**
Italy was one of the six founder members of the European Economic Community (or Common Market) in 1957. The EEC now has 12 members and is the world's largest trading bloc.

Australia 10,900

Belgium 11,360

Canada 15,080

France 12,860

West Germany 14,460

Italy 10,420

Japan 15,770

Netherlands 11,860

New Zealand 8,230

Spain 6,010

UK 10,430

USA 18,430

(in US dollars)

△ **National wealth created per person in 1987**
Italy has less wealth per person than many other industrial nations. However, Spain and some of the other Mediterranean countries are poorer still.

Denmark

Ireland

United Kingdom

Netherlands

Belgium

Lux.

W. Germany

France

Portugal

Spain

Italy

Greece

Index